EASY POP SONGS FOR ACCORDION

2   At Last

6   Blowin' in the Wind

9   Come Together

12 Don't Know Why

16 Every Breath You Take

21 Imagine

24 Mia & Sebastian's Theme

26 A Million Dreams

32 The Pink Panther

38 Raindrops Keep Fallin' on My Head

35 Scarborough Fair

46 Somewhere Out There

50 The Sound of Music

42 Stay with Me

54 Strangers in the Night

57 Sweet Caroline

62 Tomorrow

65 Viva La Vida

72 What a Wonderful World

76 With a Little Help from My Friends

Arranged by Peter Deneff

ISBN 978-1-5400-9424-7

Visit Hal Leonard Online at
www.halleonard.com

World headquarters, contact:
Hal Leonard
7777 West Bluemound Road
Milwaukee, WI 53213
Email: info@halleonard.com

In Europe, contact:
Hal Leonard Europe Limited
1 Red Place
London, W1K 6PL
Email: info@halleonardeurope.com

In Australia, contact:
Hal Leonard Australia Pty. Ltd.
4 Lentara Court
Cheltenham, Victoria, 3192 Australia
Email: info@halleonard.com.au

AT LAST
from ORCHESTRA WIVES

Lyric by MACK GORDON
Music by HARRY WARREN

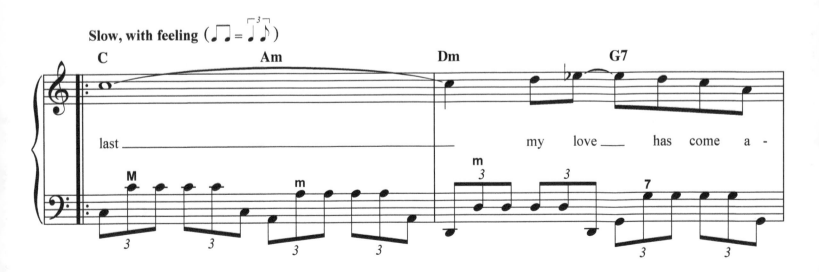

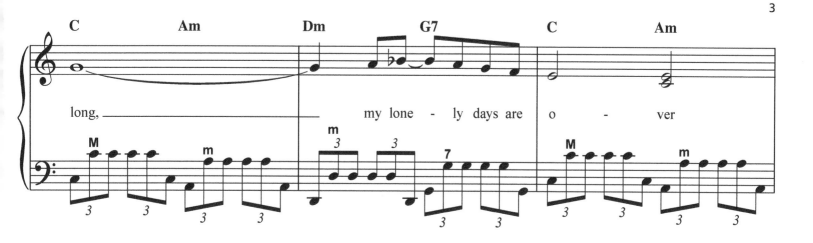

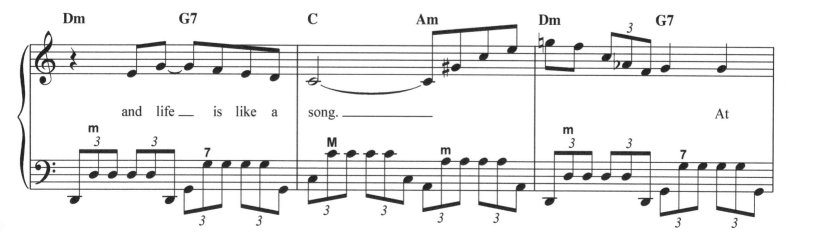

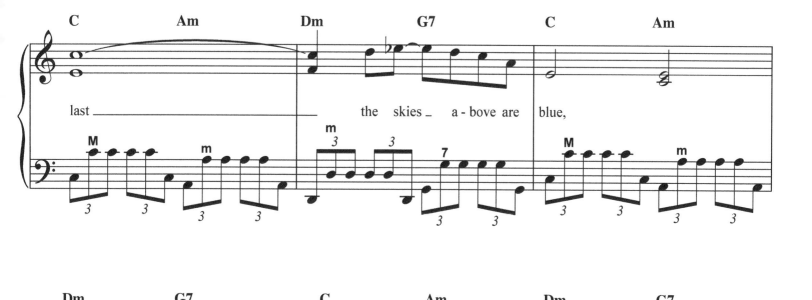

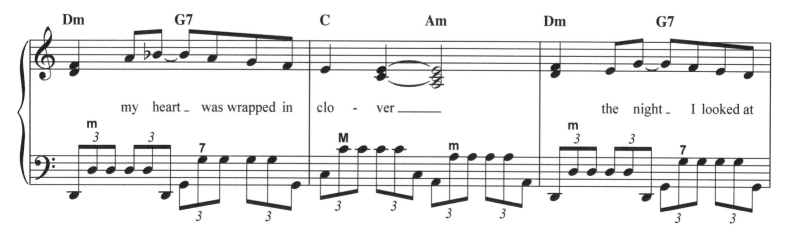

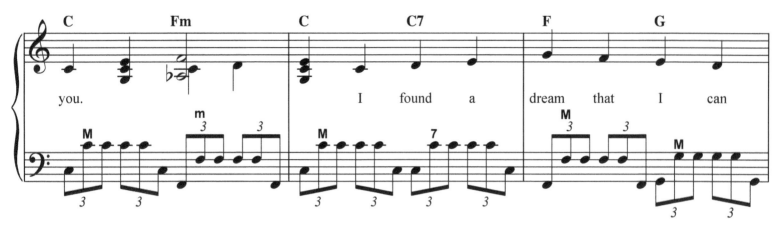

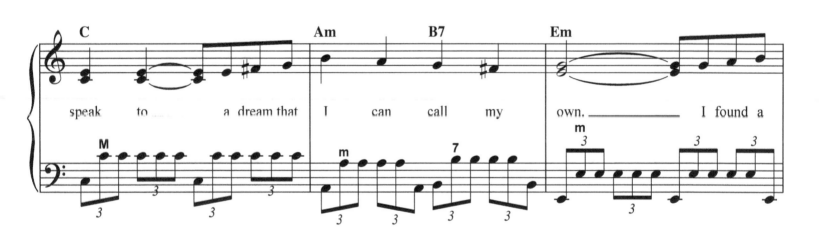

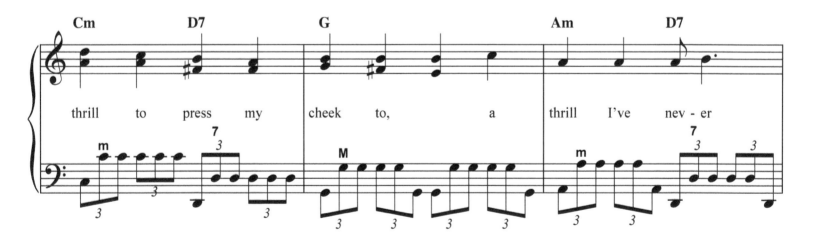

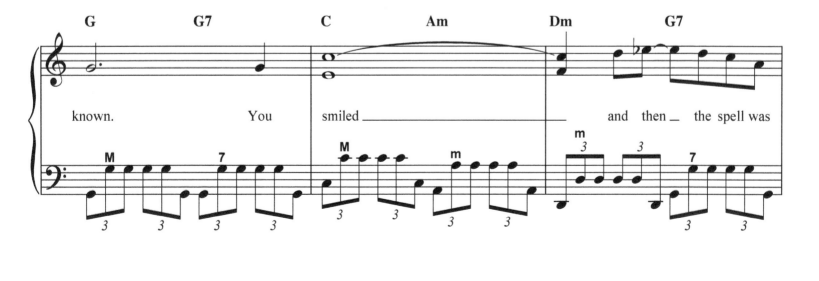

cast ... and here __ we are in heav - en

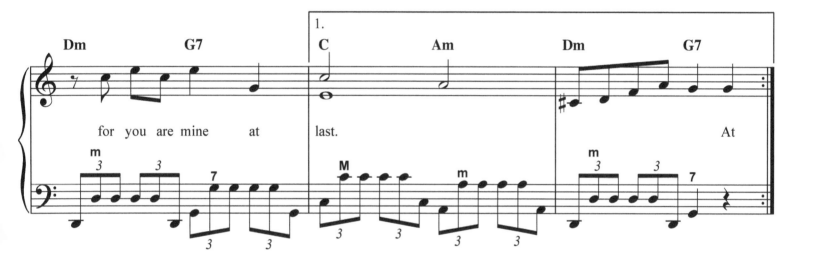

for you are mine at last. At

last.

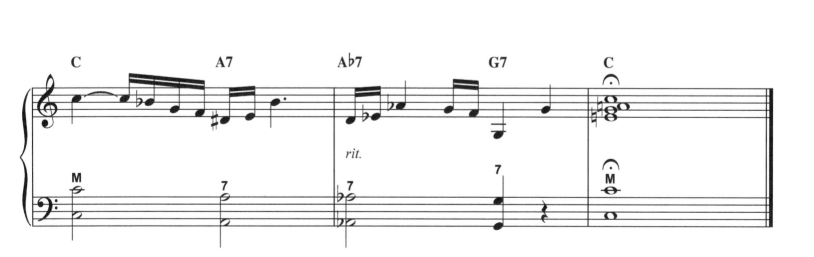

rit.

BLOWIN' IN THE WIND

Words and Music by
BOB DYLAN

Moderately fast

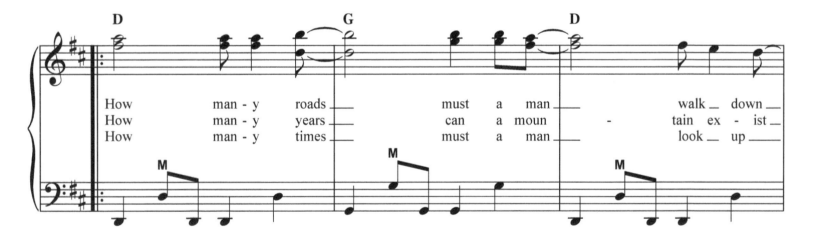

How | man - y | roads | must a man | walk down
How | man - y | years | can a moun - | tain ex - ist
How | man - y | times | must a man | look up

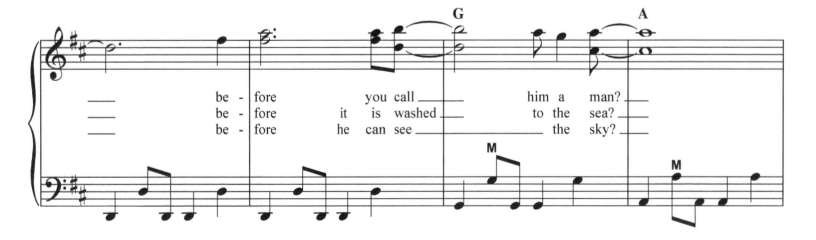

be - fore | you call | him a man?
be - fore | it is washed | to the sea?
be - fore | he can see | the sky?

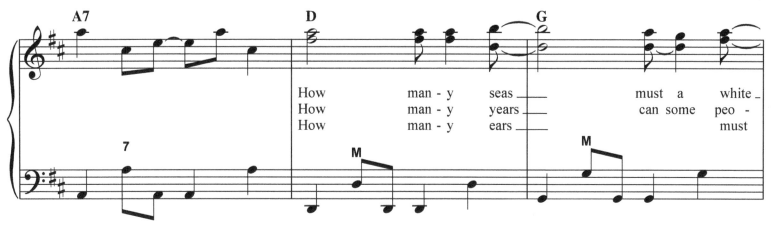

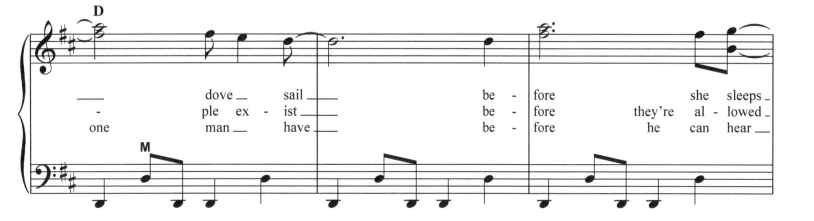

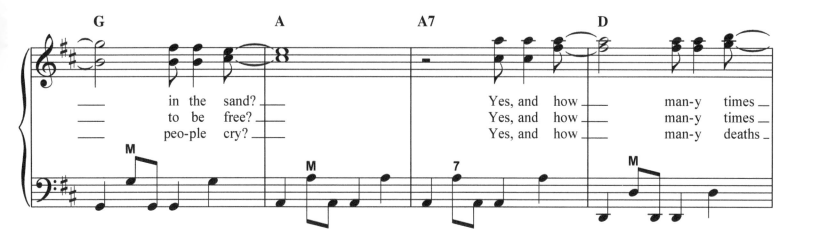

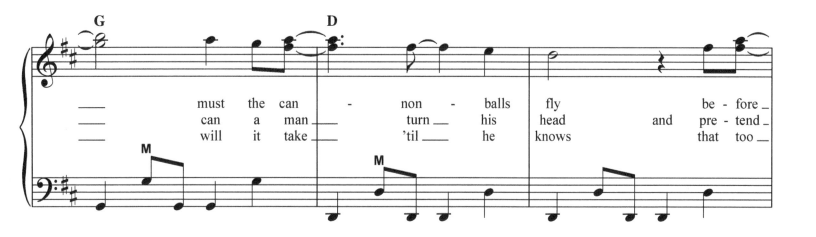

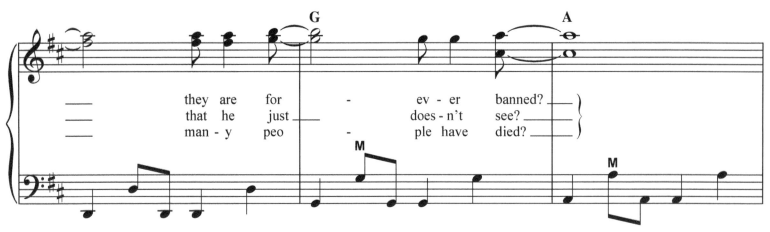

they are for - ev - er banned?
that he just - does - n't see?
man - y peo - ple have died?

The an - swer, _ my friend, is blow-in' in _ the

wind. The an - swer _ is blow - in' in _____ the

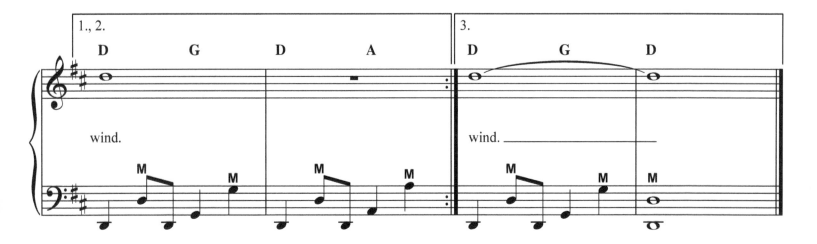

wind.

wind. _____

COME TOGETHER

Words and Music by JOHN LENNON
and PAUL McCARTNEY

Moderately slow

Here come old flat-top, he come groov-ing up slow-ly, he got

Joo Joo eye-ball, he one ho-ly roll-er, he got hair down

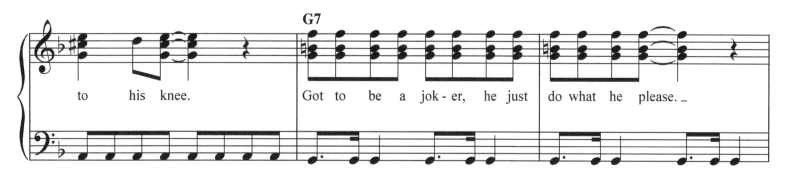

to his knee. Got to be a jok-er, he just do what he please. _

10

He wear no shoe-shine, he got toe - jam foot-ball, he got
He Bag Pro-duc - tion, he got wal - rus gum-boot, he got
He roll - er coast - er, he got ear - ly warn-ing, he got

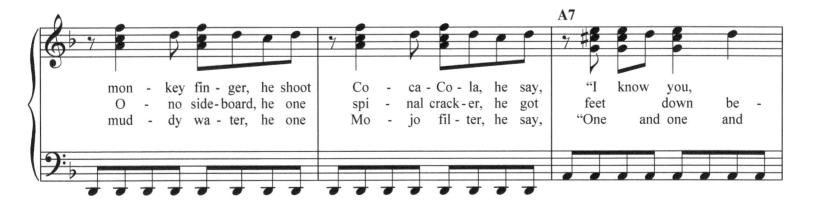

mon - key fin - ger, he shoot Co - ca - Co - la, he say, "I know you,
O - no side-board, he one spi - nal crack-er, he got feet down be -
mud - dy wa - ter, he one Mo - jo fil - ter, he say, "One and one and

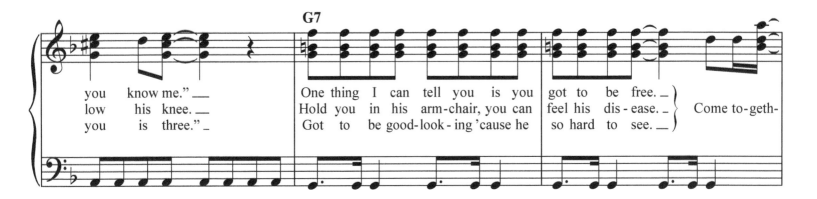

you know me." — One thing I can tell you is you got to be free. — ⎫
low his knee. — Hold you in his arm-chair, you can feel his dis - ease. — ⎬ Come to-geth-
you is three." — Got to be good-look - ing 'cause he so hard to see. — ⎭

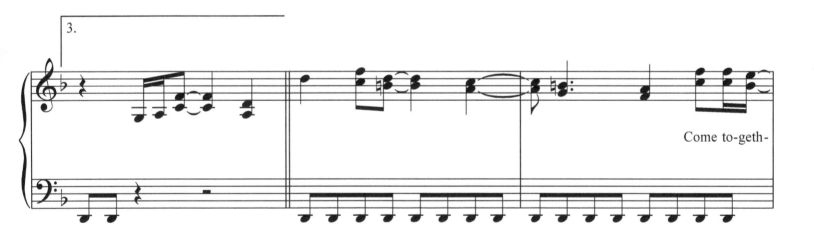

DON'T KNOW WHY

Words and Music by
JESSE HARRIS

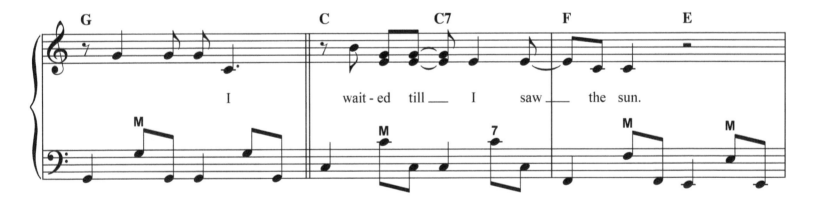

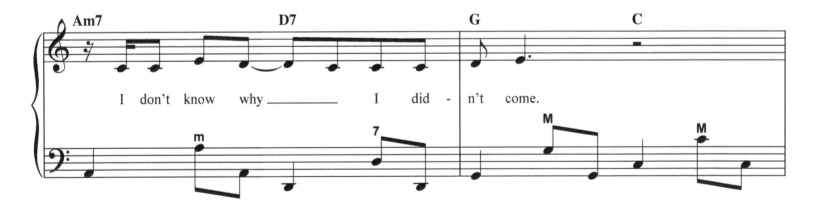

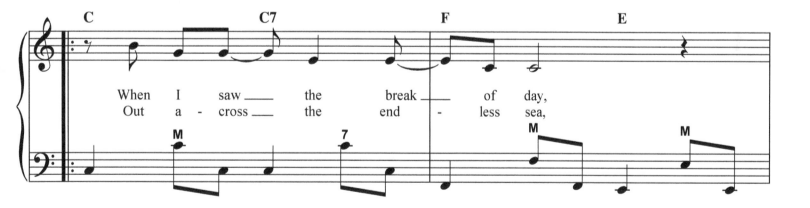

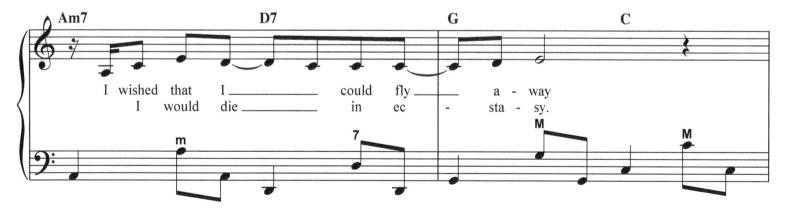

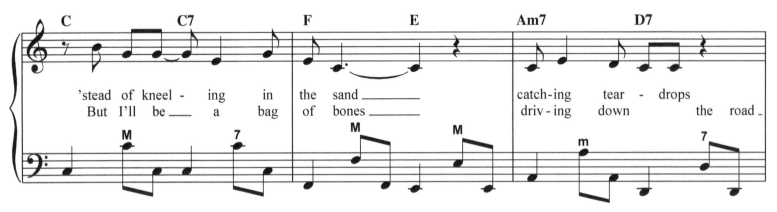

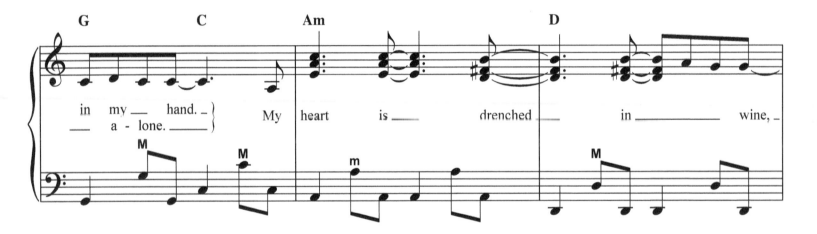

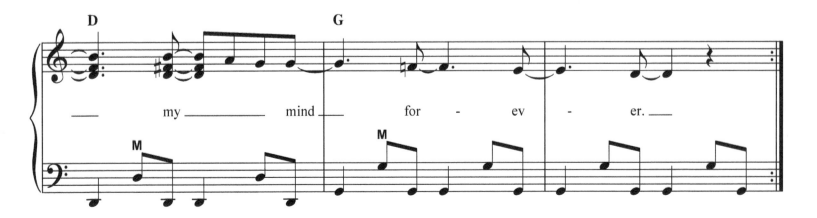

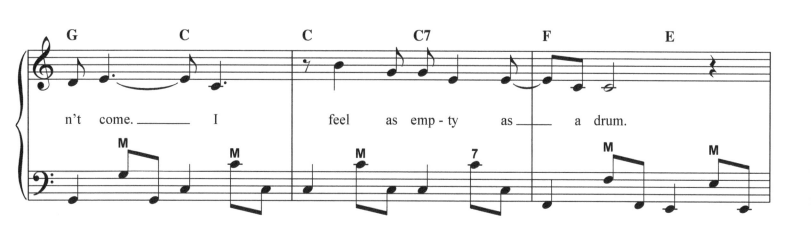

EVERY BREATH YOU TAKE

Words and Music by
STING

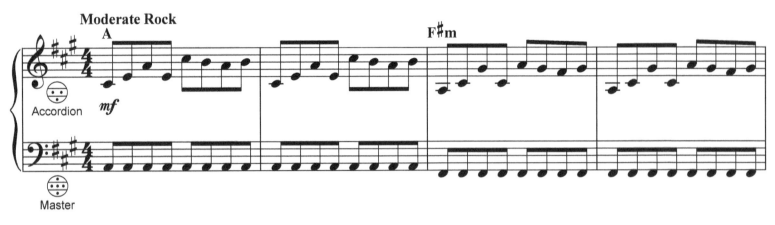

Ev-'ry breath you _

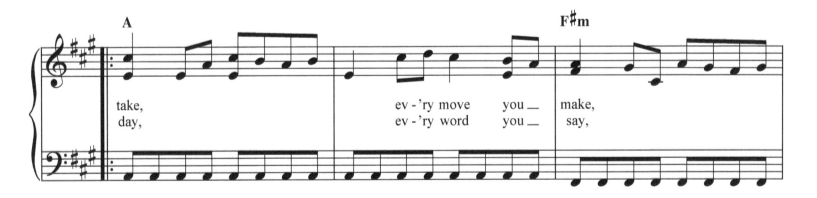

take,
day,

ev-'ry move you _ make,
ev-'ry word you _ say,

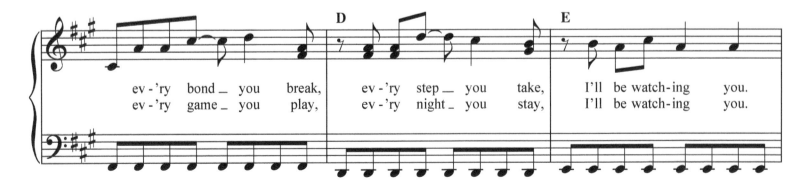

ev-'ry bond _ you break,
ev-'ry game _ you play,

ev-'ry step _ you take,
ev-'ry night _ you stay,

I'll be watch-ing you.
I'll be watch-ing you.

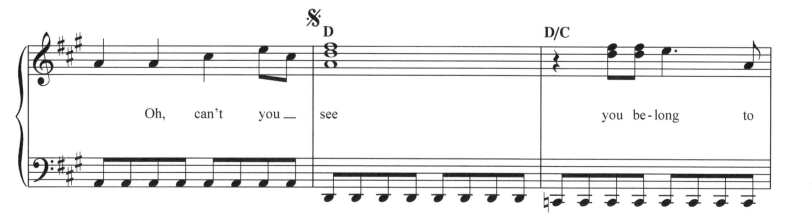

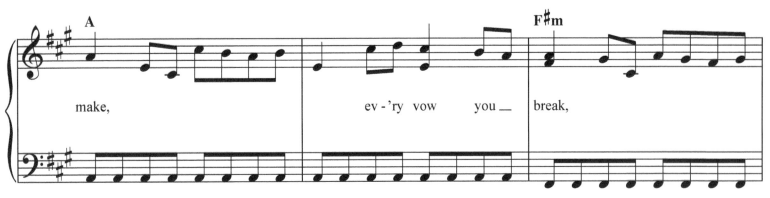

make, ev-'ry vow you __ break,

ev-'ry smile __ you fake, ev-'ry claim __ you stake, I'll be watch-ing you.

Since you've gone, __ I been lost

with - out ___ a trace, I dream at night I can on - ly see __ your face.

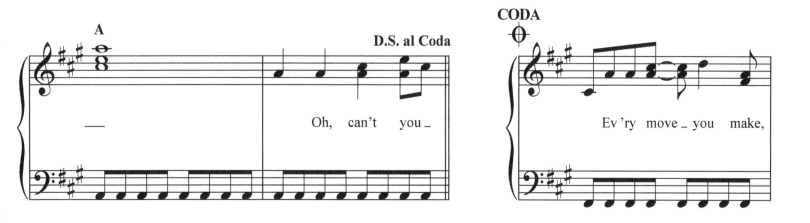

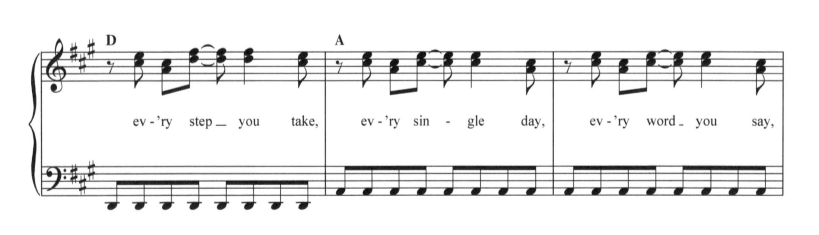

IMAGINE

Words and Music by
JOHN LENNON

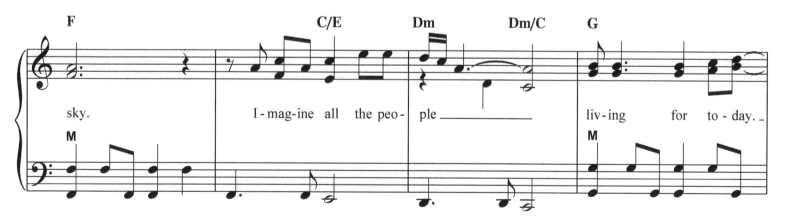

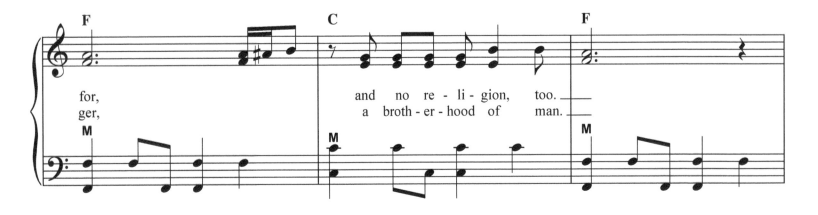

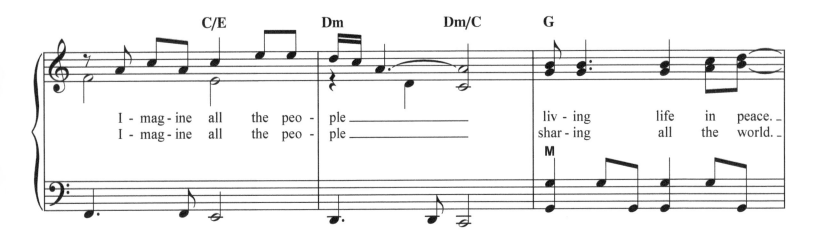

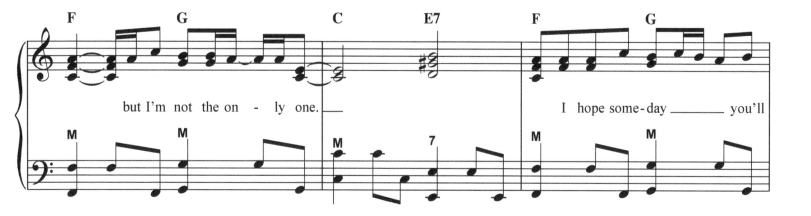

MIA & SEBASTIAN'S THEME

from LA LA LAND

Music by
JUSTIN HURWITZ

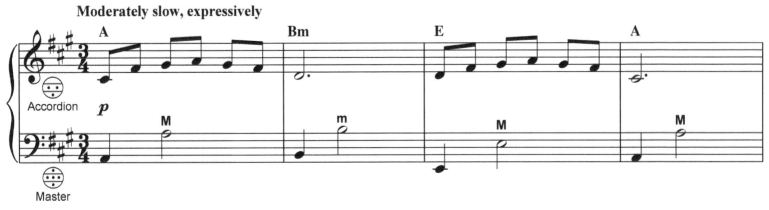

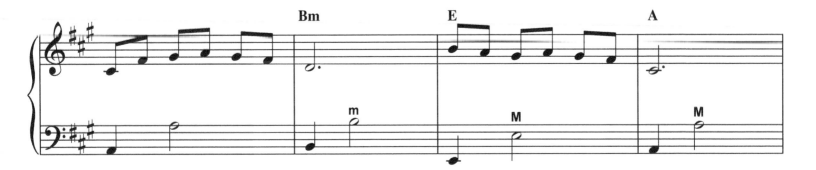

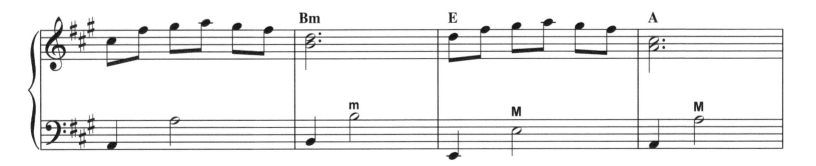

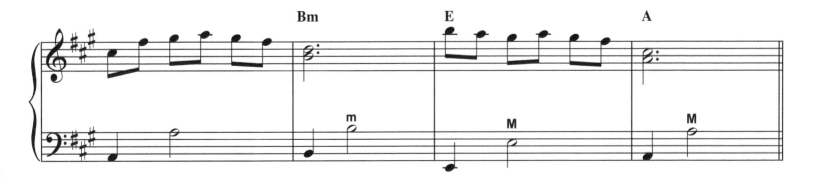

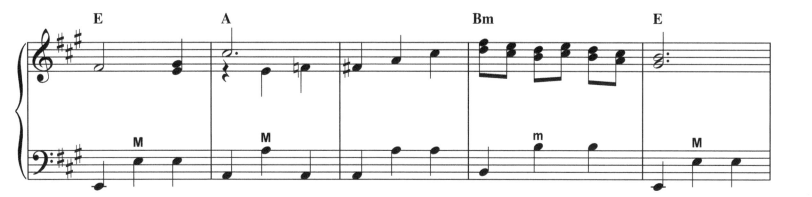

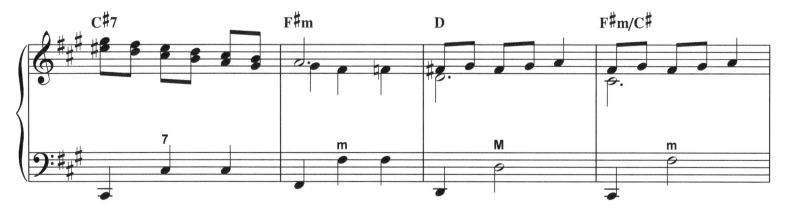

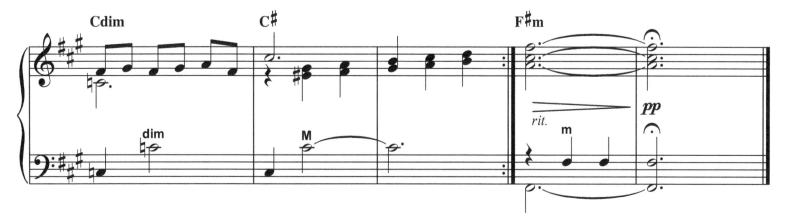

A MILLION DREAMS
from THE GREATEST SHOWMAN

Words and Music by BENJ PASEK
and JUSTIN PAUL

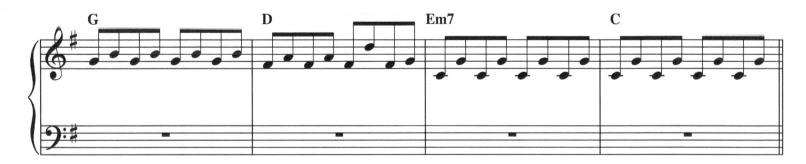

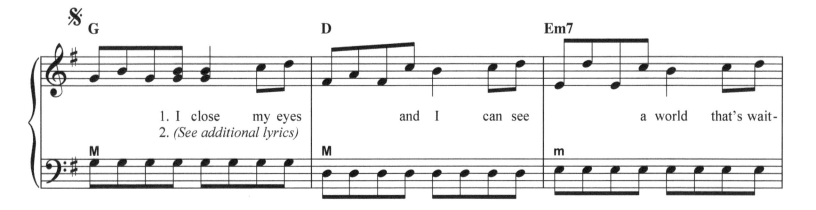

1. I close my eyes and I can see a world that's wait-
2. (See additional lyrics)

-ing up for me that I call my

own

Through the dark,

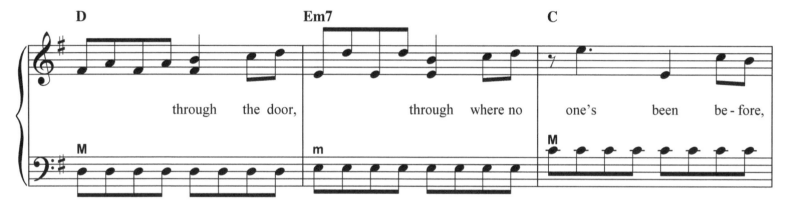

through the door, through where no one's been be-fore,

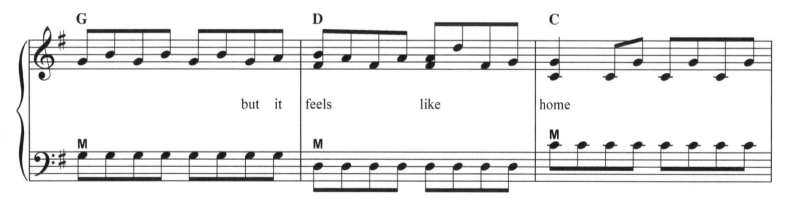

but it feels like home

Pre-Chorus

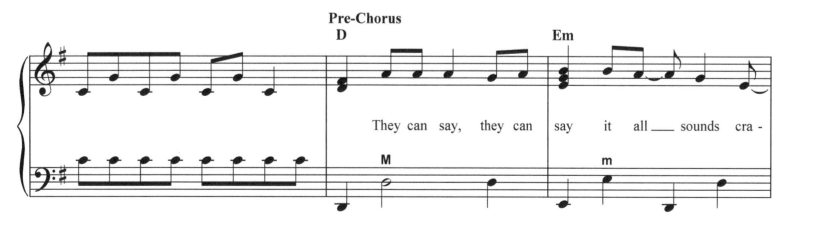

They can say, they can say it all __ sounds cra-

28

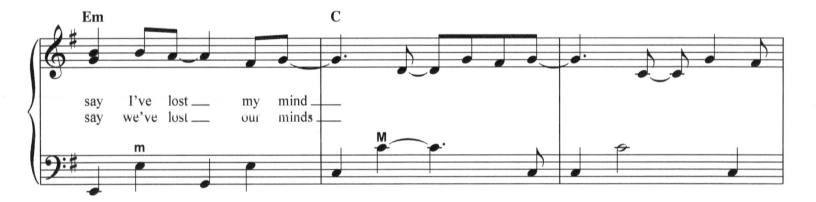

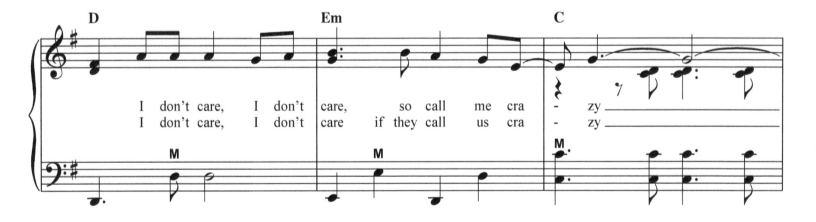

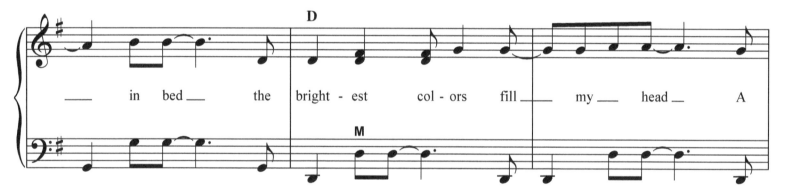

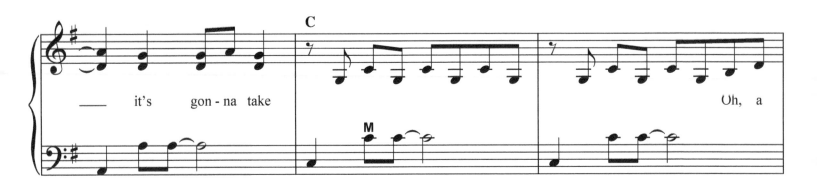

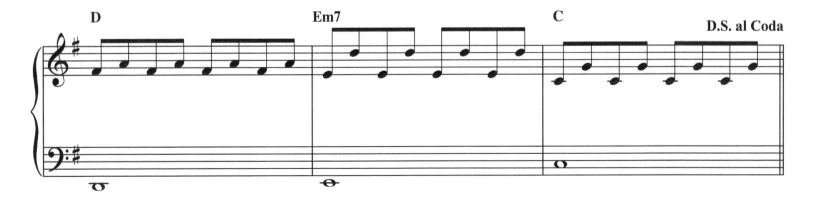

CODA

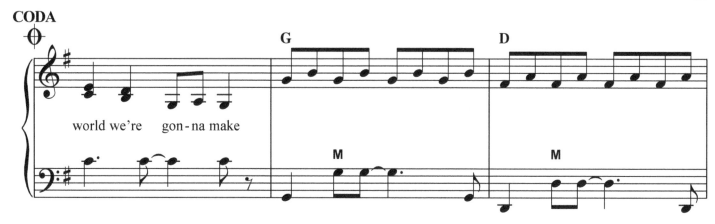

world we're gon-na make

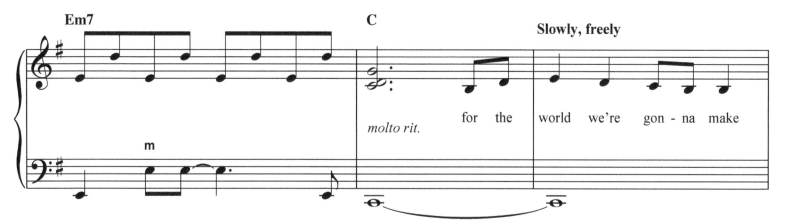

molto rit.   for   the   world   we're   gon - na   make

Slowly, freely

Additional Lyrics

2. There's a house we can build
   Ev'ry room inside is filled with things from far away
   Special things I compile,
   Each one there to make you smile on a rainy day
   (Pre-Chorus)

THE PINK PANTHER
from THE PINK PANTHER

By HENRY MANCINI

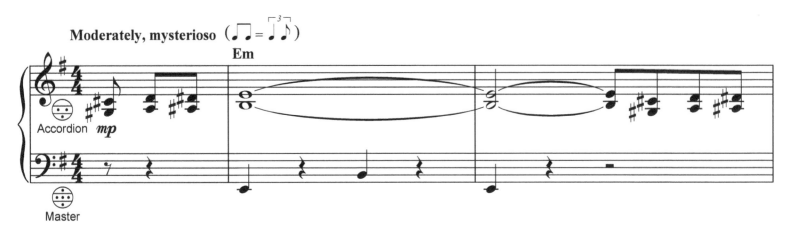

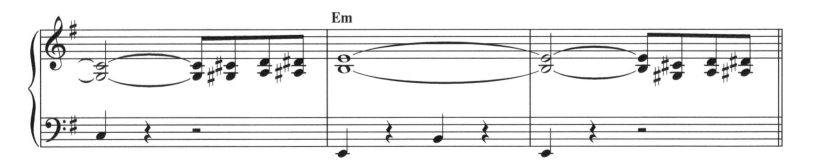

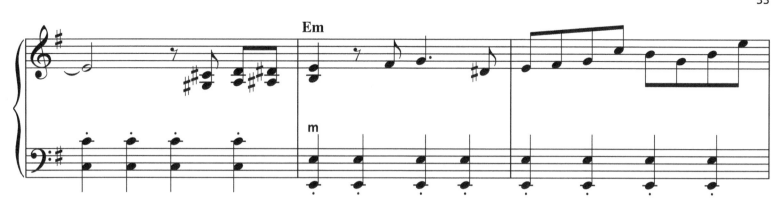

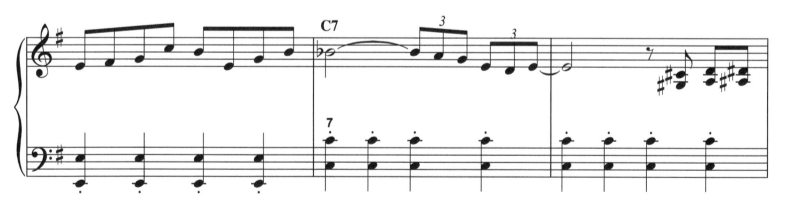

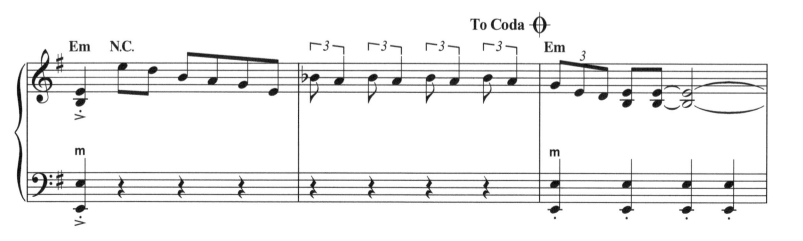

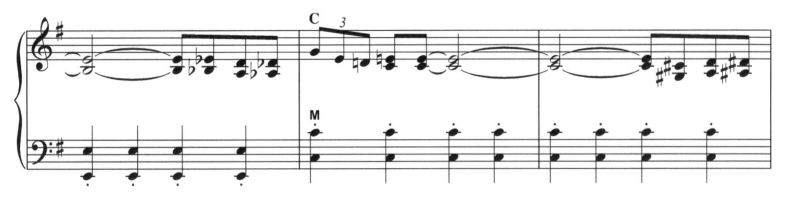

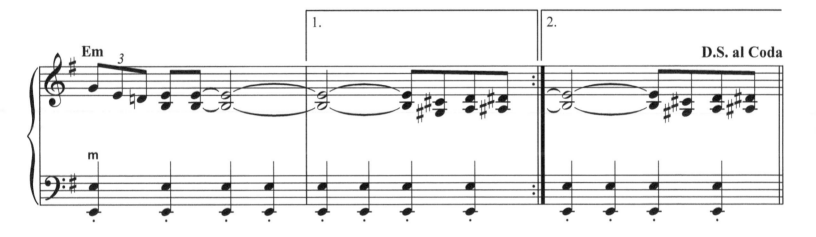

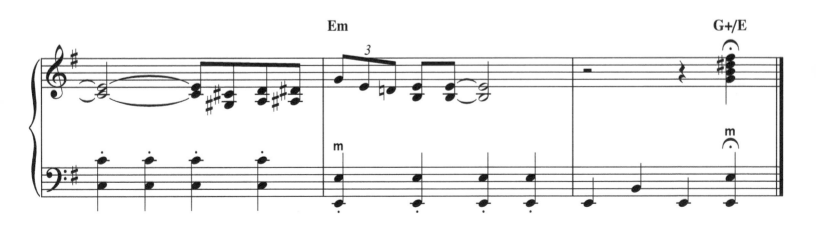

SCARBOROUGH FAIR

Traditional English

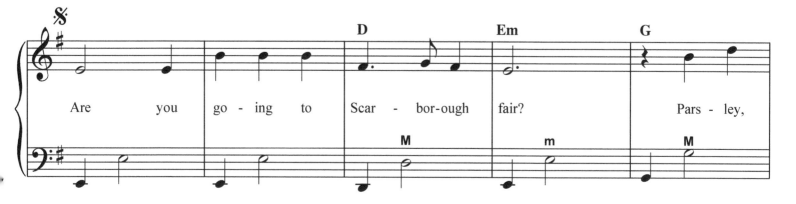

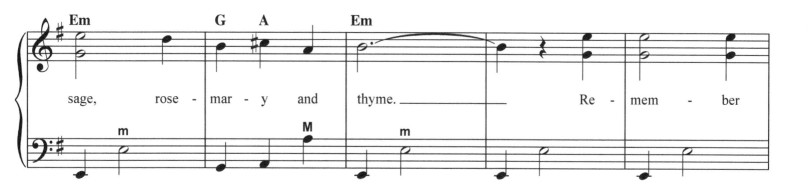

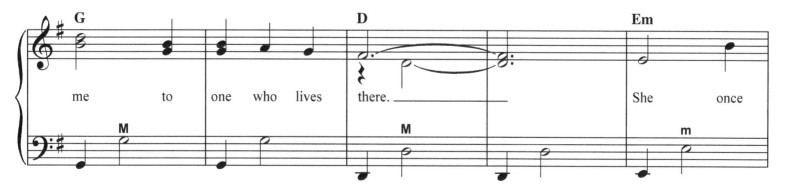

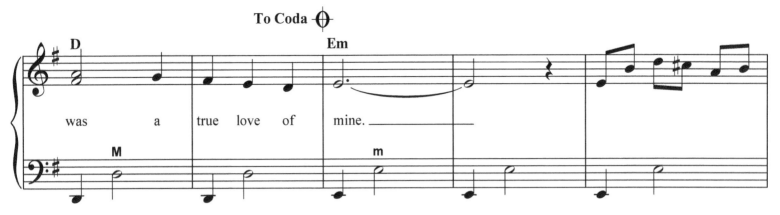

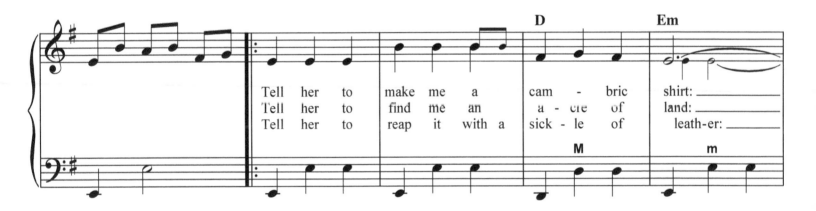

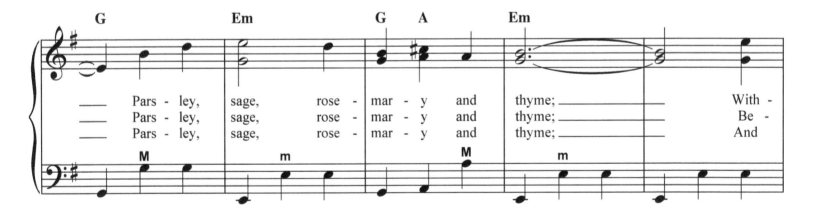

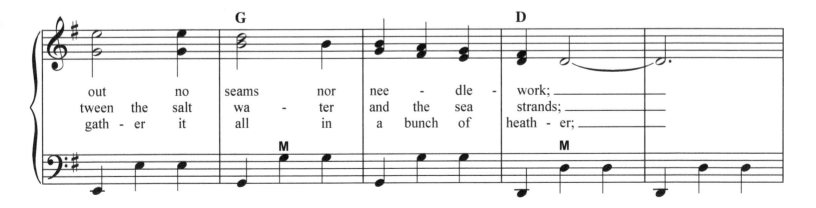

Then she'll be a true love of mine. _____
Then she'll be a true love of mine. _____
Then she'll be a true love of mine. _____

1., 2.

3.

D.S. al Coda

CODA

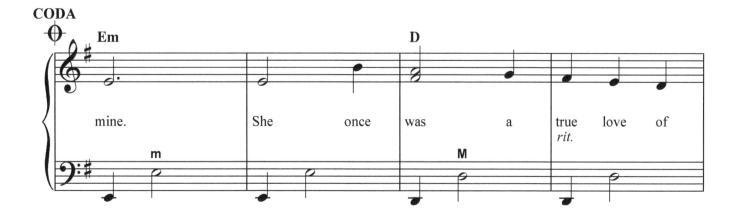

mine. She once was a true love of
rit.

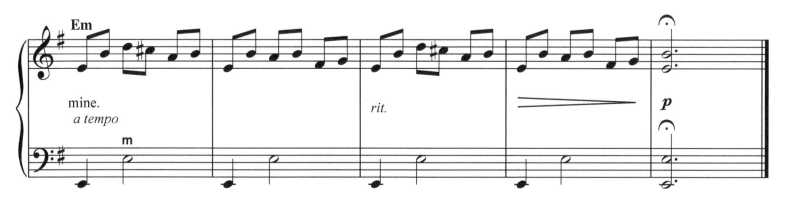

mine.
a tempo

rit.

p

RAINDROPS KEEP FALLING ON MY HEAD

from BUTCH CASSIDY AND THE SUNDANCE KID

Lyrics by HAL DAVID
Music by BURT BACHARACH

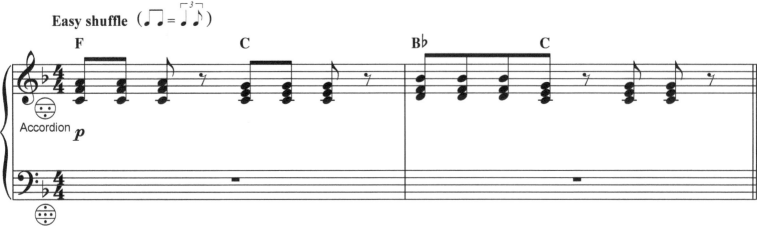

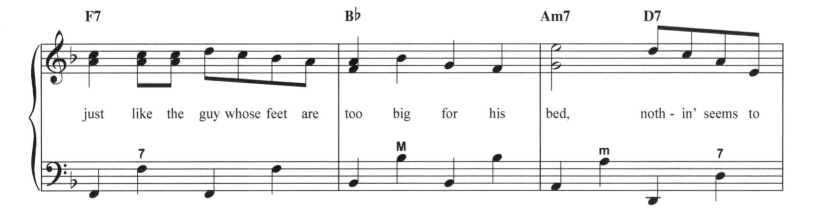

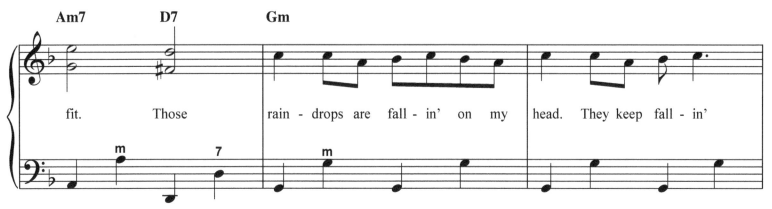

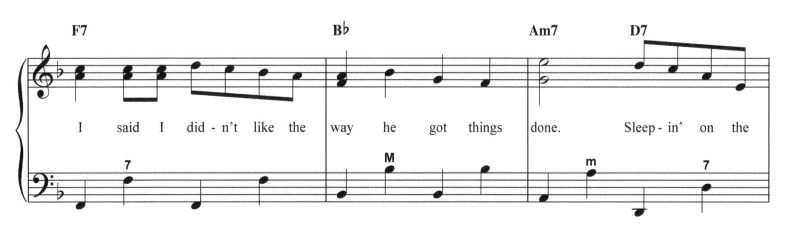

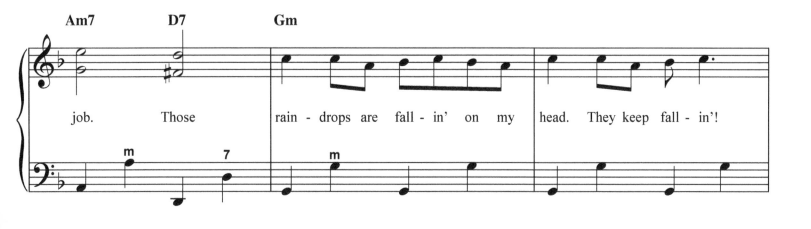

But there's one thing I know: ___ the

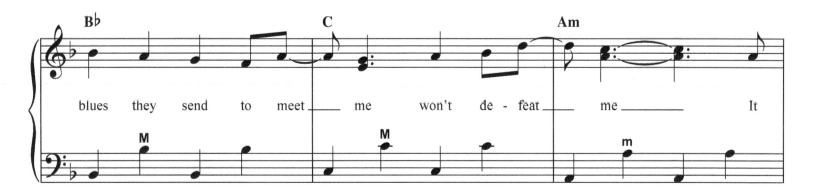

blues they send to meet ___ me won't de - feat ___ me ___ It

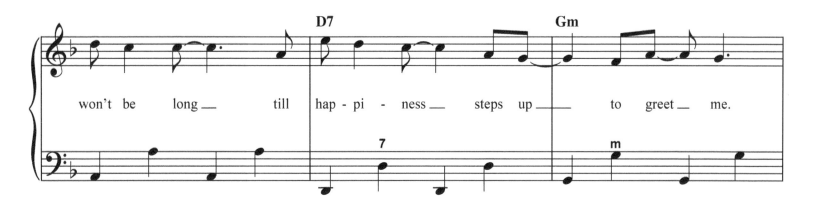

won't be long ___ till hap - pi - ness ___ steps up ___ to greet ___ me.

Rain - drops keep fall - in' on my

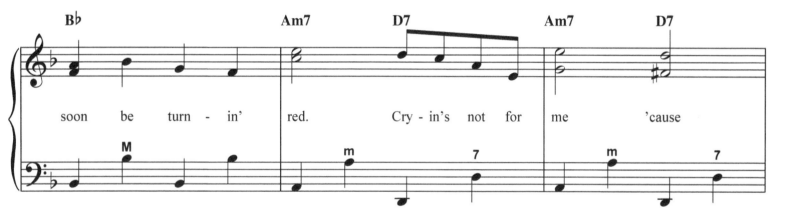

STAY WITH ME

Words and Music by SAM SMITH,
JAMES NAPIER, WILLIAM EDWARD PHILLIPS,
TOM PETTY and JEFF LYNNE

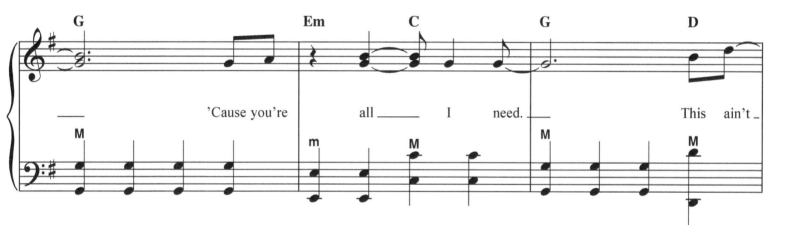

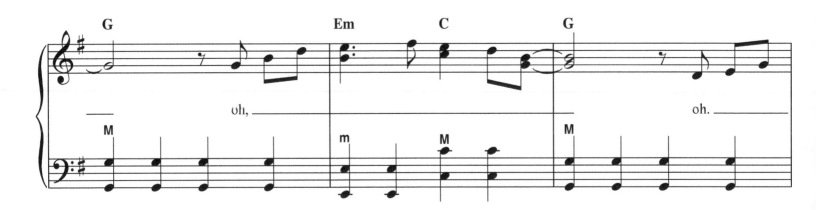

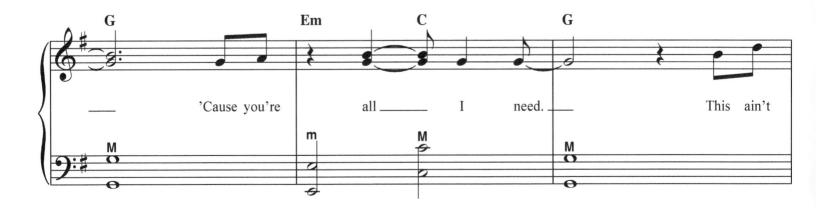

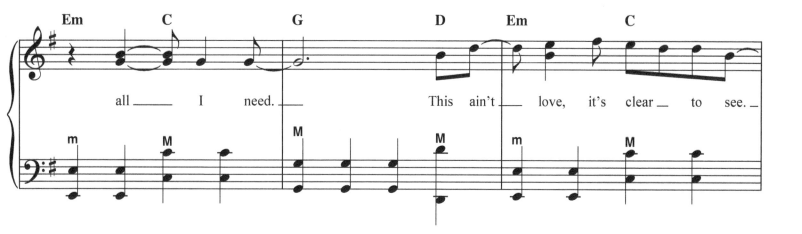

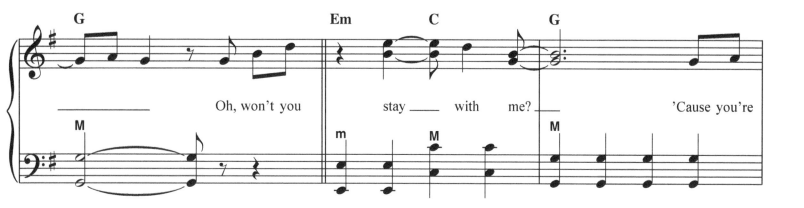

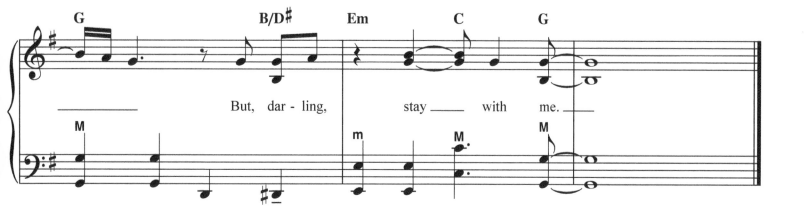

SOMEWHERE OUT THERE
from AN AMERICAN TAIL

Music by BARRY MANN and JAMES HORNER
Lyric by CYNTHIA WEIL

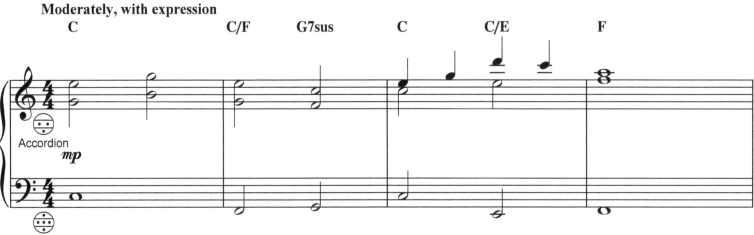

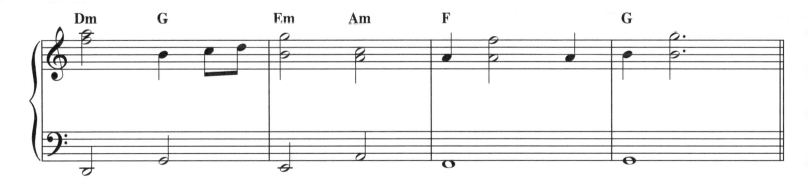

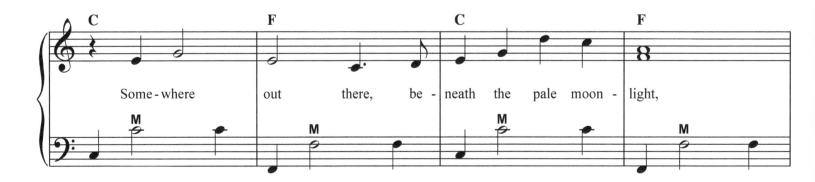

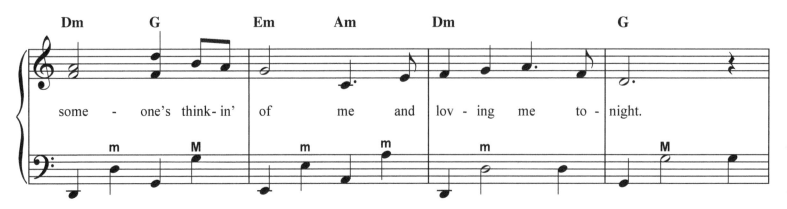

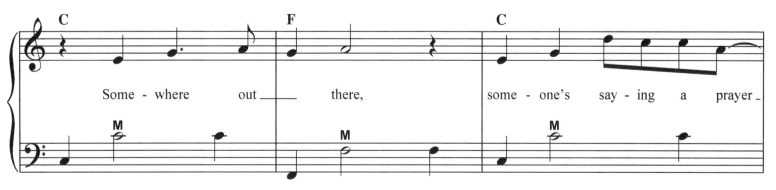

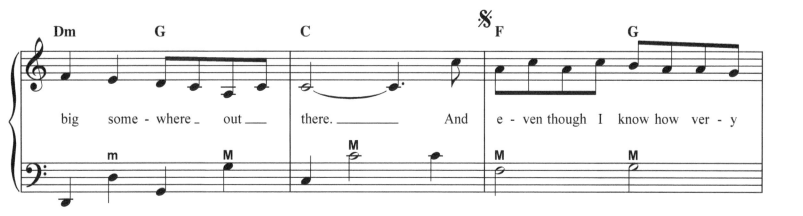

48

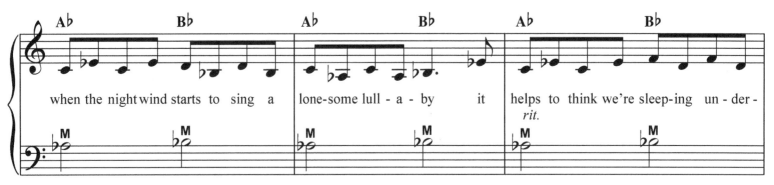

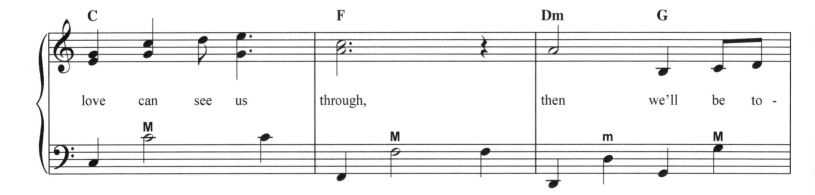

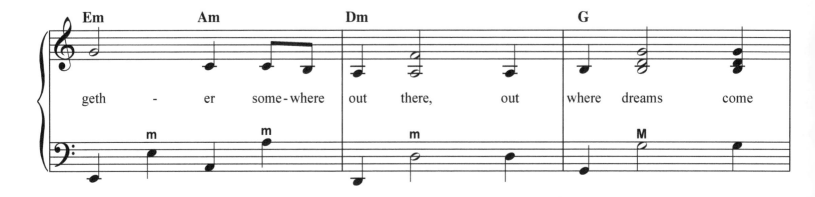

true.

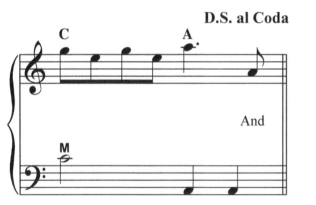

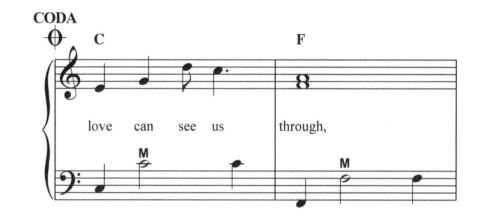

And

love can see us through,

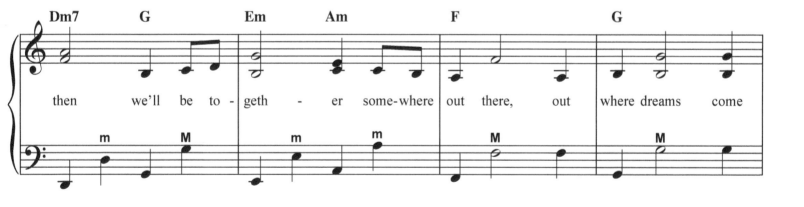

then we'll be to-geth-er some-where out there, out where dreams come

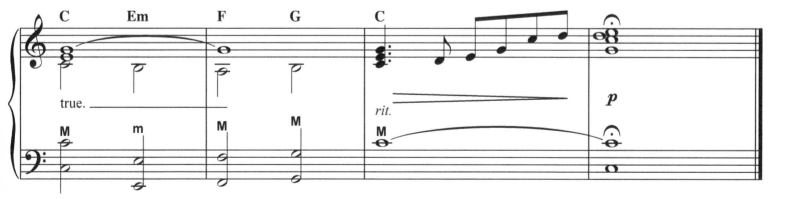

true.

THE SOUND OF MUSIC

from THE SOUND OF MUSIC

Lyrics by OSCAR HAMMERSTEIN II
Music by RICHARD RODGERS

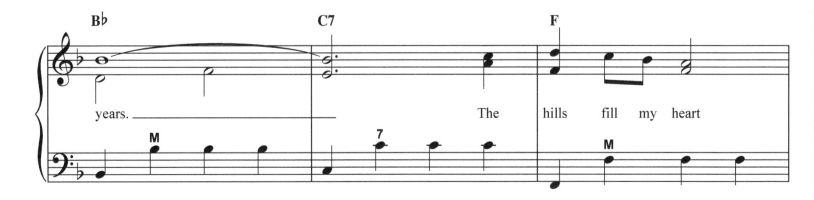

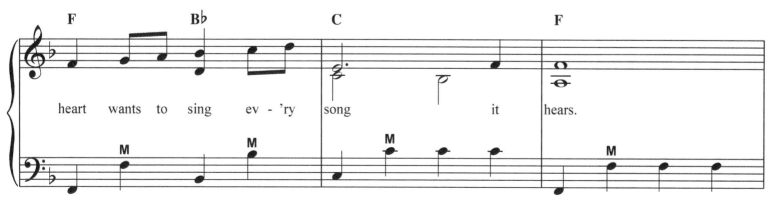

heart wants to sing ev - 'ry song it hears.

My heart wants to beat like the wings of the birds that rise from the

lake to the trees. My heart wants to sigh like a

chime that flies from a church on a breeze, to

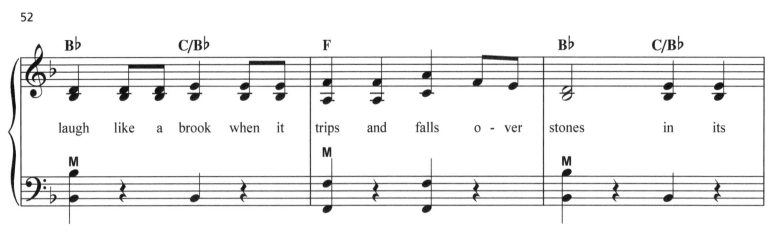

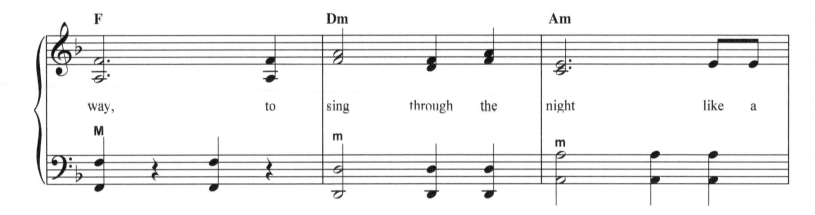

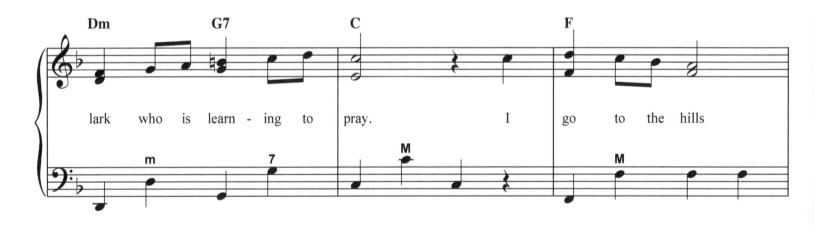

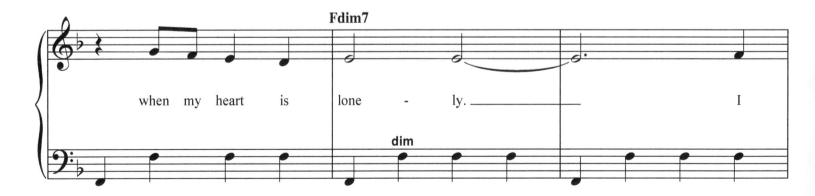

know I will hear what I've heard be - fore. _____

_____ My heart will be blessed with the sound of

mu - sic _____ and I'll sing

once more.

STRANGERS IN THE NIGHT
adapted from A MAN COULD GET KILLED

Words by CHARLES SINGLETON and EDDIE SNYDER
Music by BERT KAEMPFERT

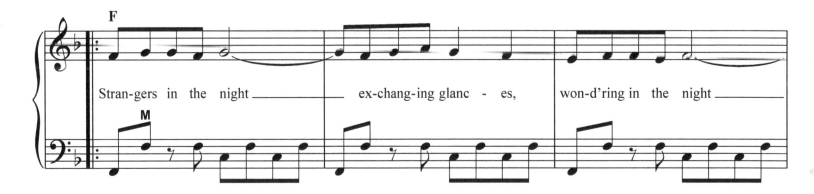

Stran-gers in the night _____ ex-chang-ing glanc - es, won-d'ring in the night _____

_____ what were the chanc - es we'd be shar-ing love _____ be-fore the night was

through. _____ Some-thing in your eyes _____

55

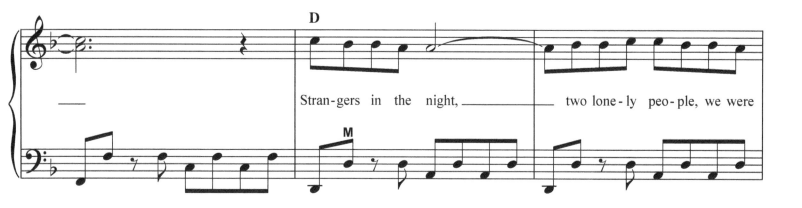

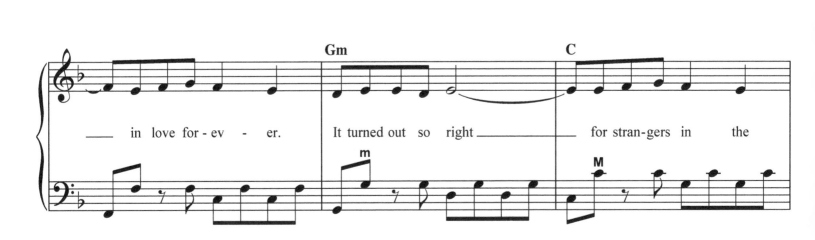

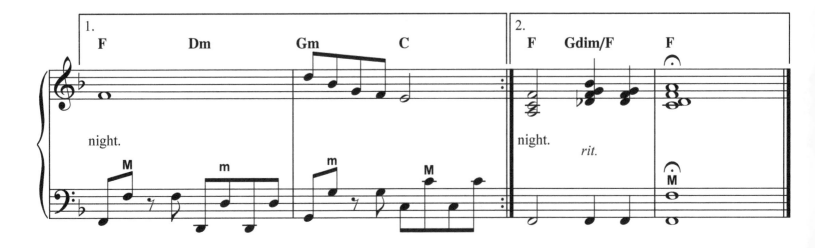

SWEET CAROLINE

Words and Music by
NEIL DIAMOND

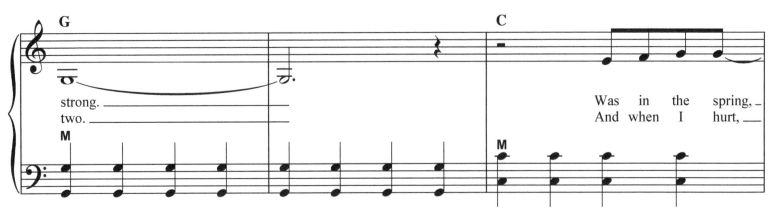

strong. _____
two. _____

Was in the spring, _
And when I hurt, ____

and spring be - came the sum - mer.
hurt - in' runs off my shoul - ders.

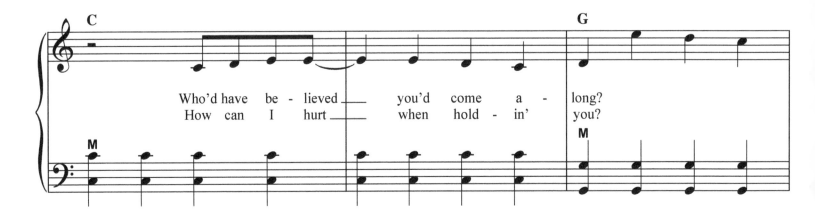

Who'd have be - lieved ___ you'd come a - long?
How can I hurt ___ when hold - in' you?

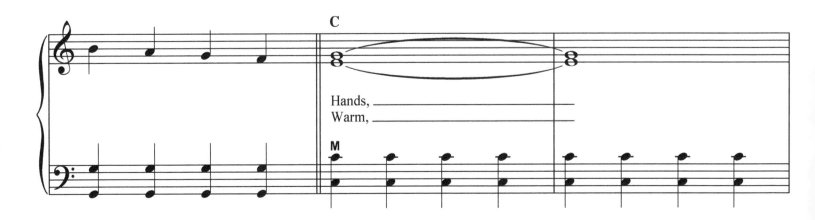

Hands, _____
Warm, _____

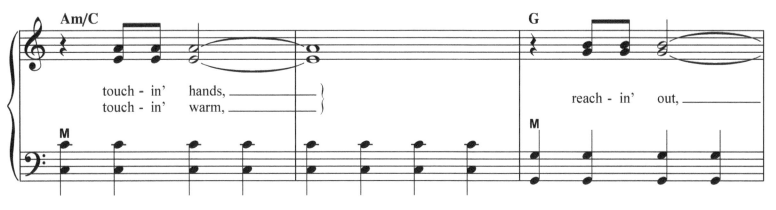

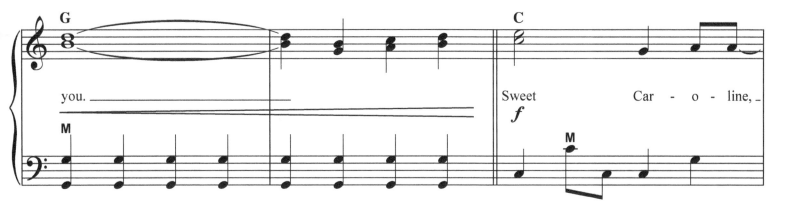

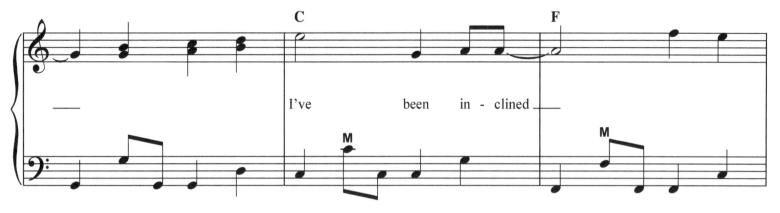

I've been in-clined

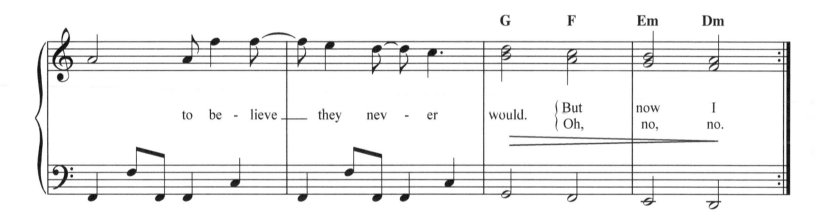

to be - lieve they nev - er would. { But now I
{ Oh, no, no.

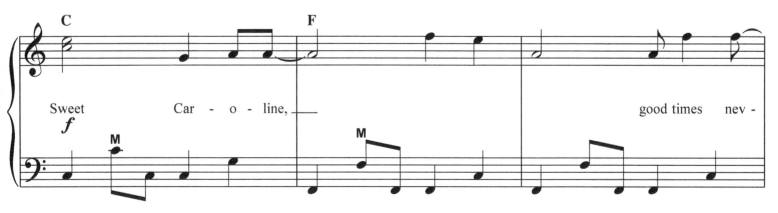

Sweet Car - o - line, ___ good times nev -

- er seemed so good.

I've been in - clined ___ to be - lieve _

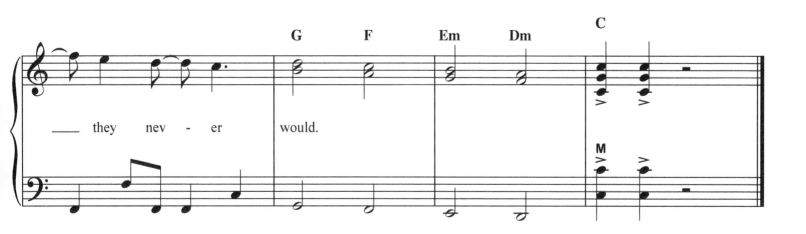

__ they nev - er would.

TOMORROW
from the Musical Production ANNIE

Lyric by MARTIN CHARNIN
Music by CHARLES STROUSE

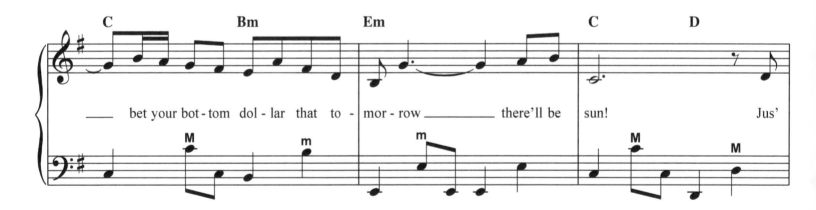

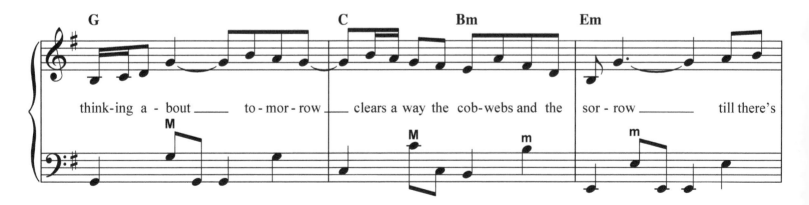

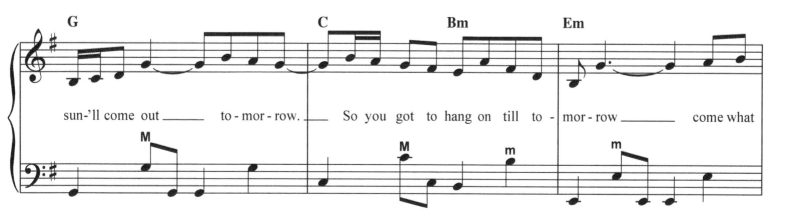

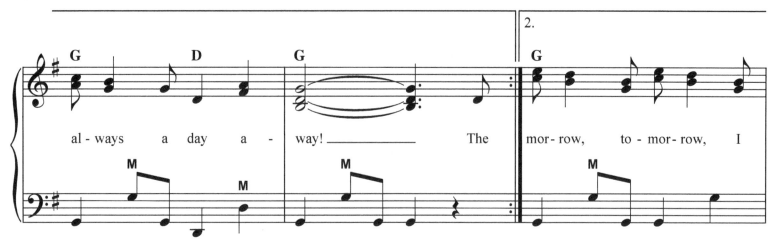

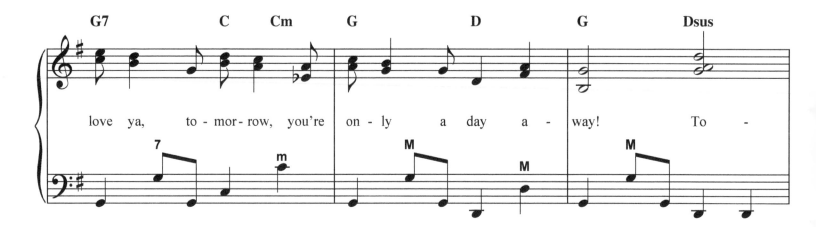

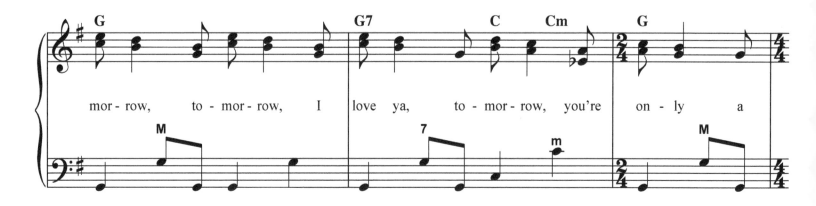

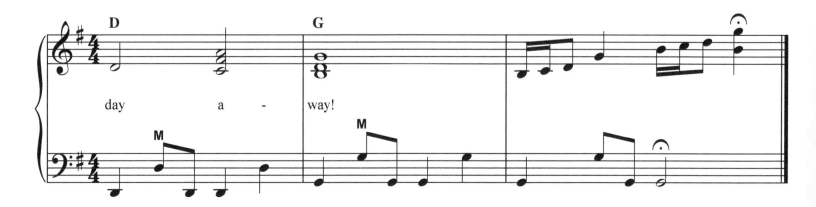

VIVA LA VIDA

Words and Music by GUY BERRYMAN,
JON BUCKLAND, WILL CHAMPION
and CHRIS MARTIN

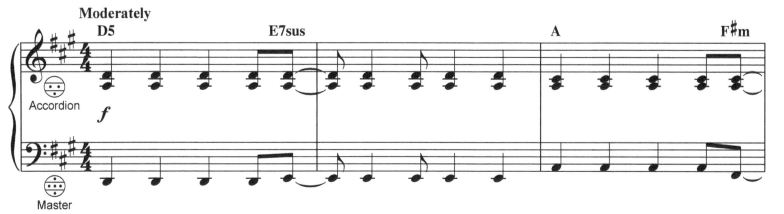

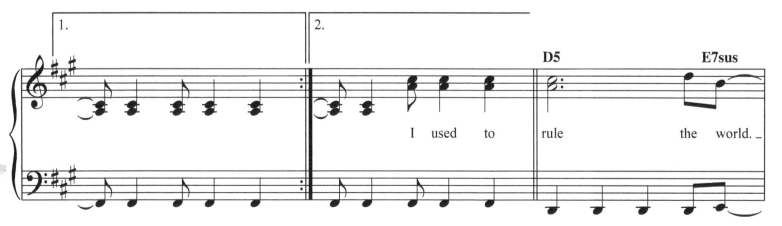

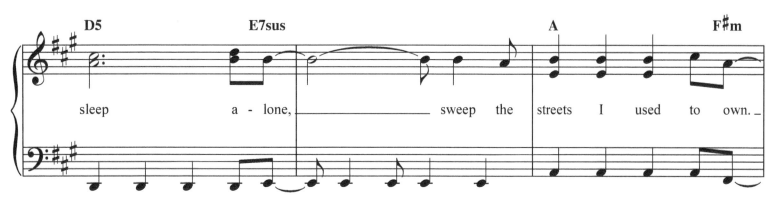

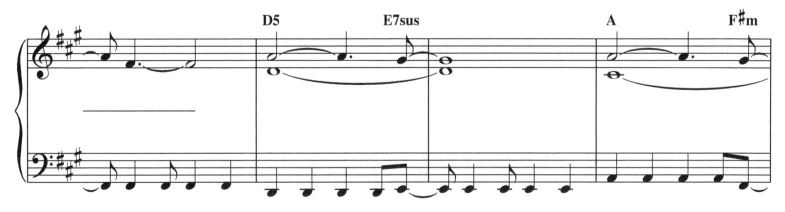

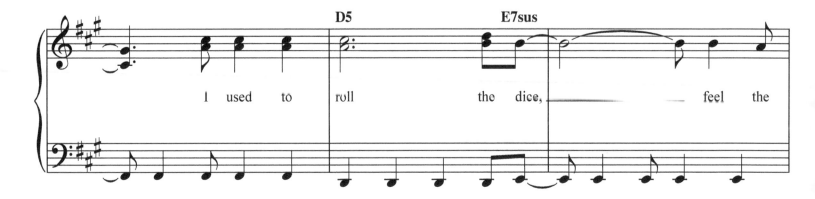

I used to roll the dice, ___ feel the

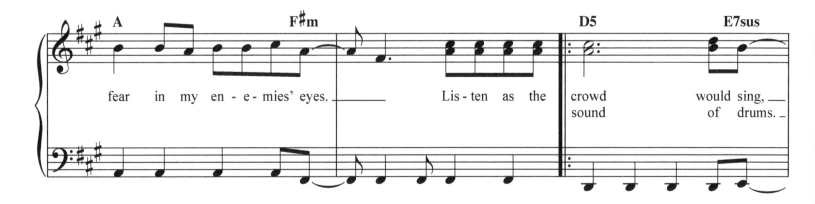

fear in my en-e-mies' eyes. ___ Lis-ten as the crowd would sing, ___
sound of drums. ___

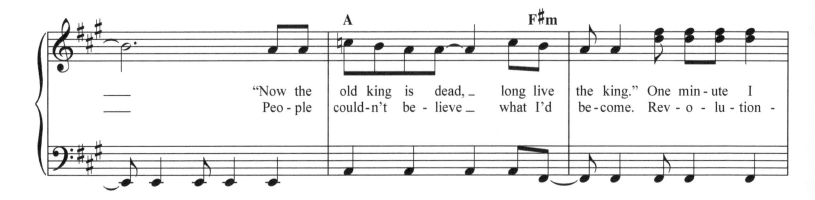

___ "Now the old king is dead, ___ long live the king." One min-ute I
___ Peo-ple could-n't be-lieve ___ what I'd be-come. Rev-o-lu-tion-

held the key, next the walls were closed on
ar - ies wait for my head on a sil - ver

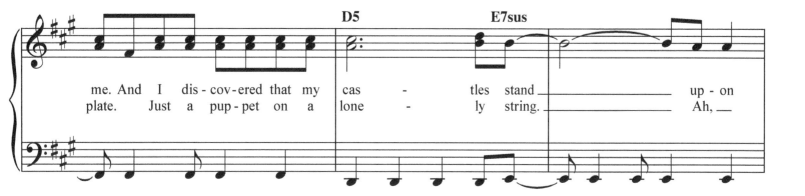

me. And I dis-cov-ered that my cas - tles stand up-on
plate. Just a pup-pet on a lone - ly string. Ah,

pil-lars of salt and pil-lars of sand. I hear
who would ev-er wan-na be king? I hear Je-ru-sa-lem bells
(D.S.) Hear

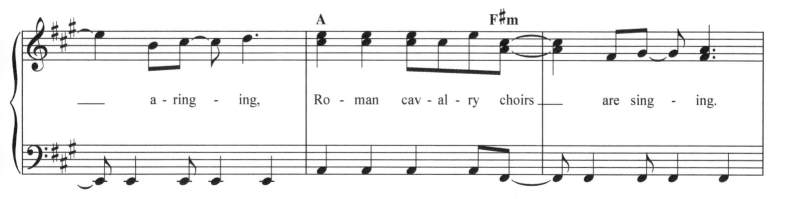

 a-ring-ing, Ro-man cav-al-ry choirs are sing-ing.

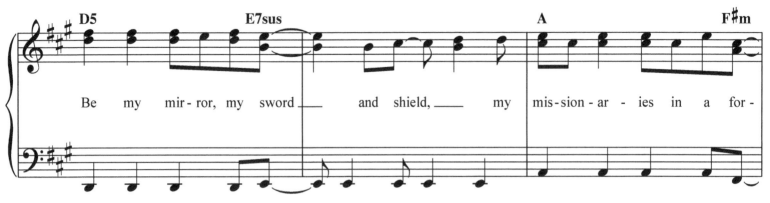

Be my mir - ror, my sword ___ and shield, ___ my mis - sion - ar - ies in a for-

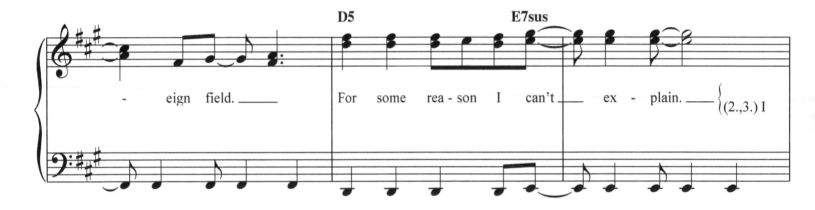

- eign field. ___ For some rea - son I can't ___ ex - plain. ___ {(2.,3.) I

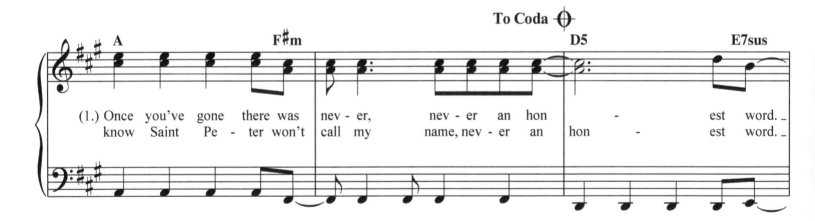

To Coda

(1.) Once you've gone there was nev - er, nev - er an hon - est word.
know Saint Pe - ter won't call my name, nev - er an hon - est word.

1.

___ And that was when I ruled the world. ___
But that was when I ruled the world. _

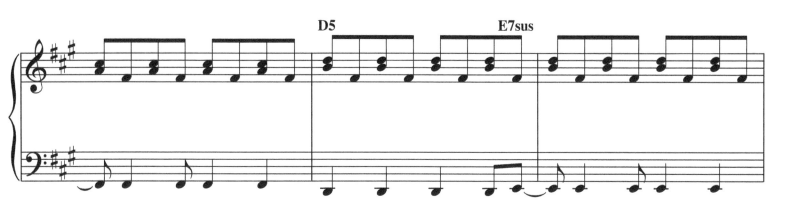

It was a wick-ed and wild _____ wind _

_____ blew down the doors to __ let me in. __ Shat-tered win-dows and the

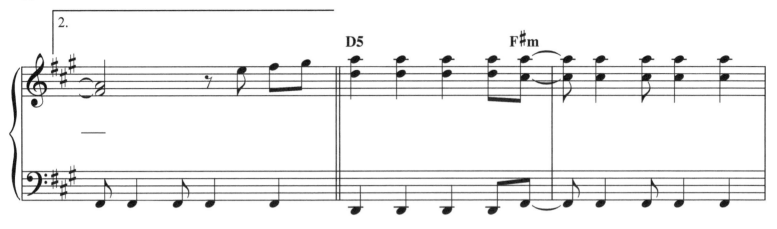

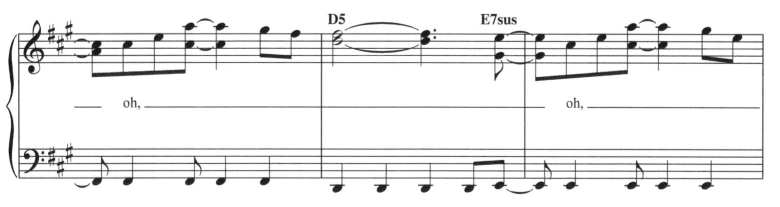

oh, _____ oh, _____

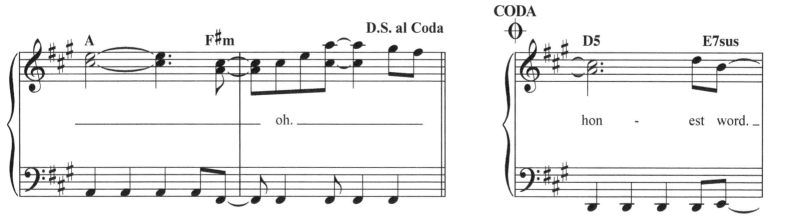

D.S. al Coda **CODA**

A F#m D5 E7sus

_____ oh. _____ hon - est word. __

A F#m D

_____ But that was when I ruled the world. ____ *mp*

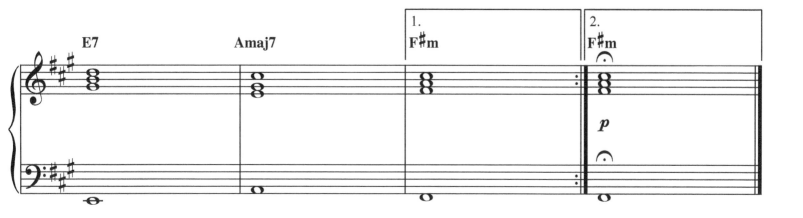

E7 Amaj7 1. F#m 2. F#m

p

WHAT A WONDERFUL WORLD

Words and Music by GEORGE DAVID WEISS
and BOB THIELE

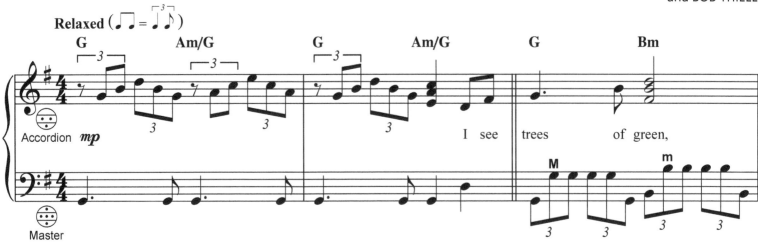

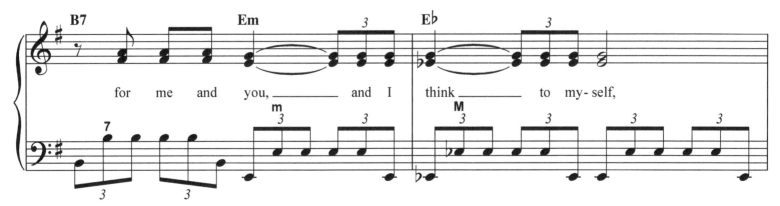

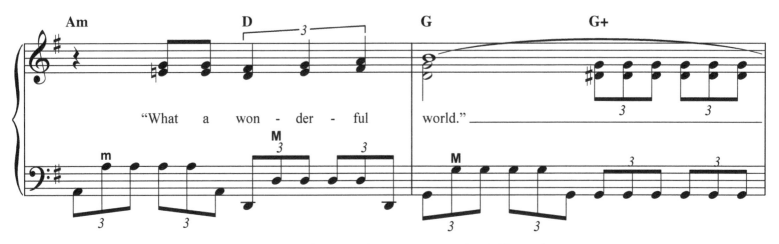

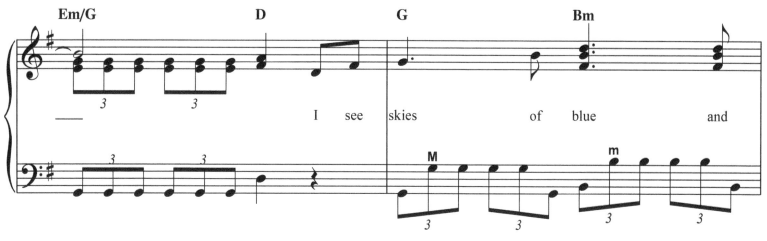

I see skies of blue and

clouds of white, the bright _____ bless-ed day, the

dark _____ sa - cred night, _____ and I think _____ to my- self,

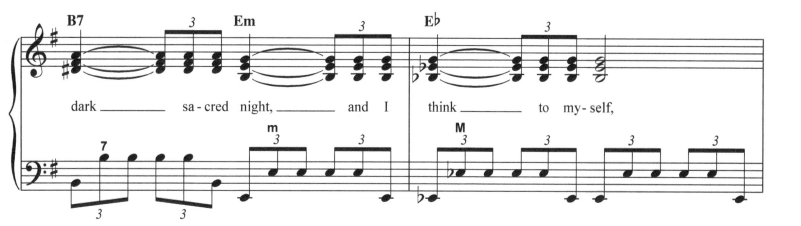

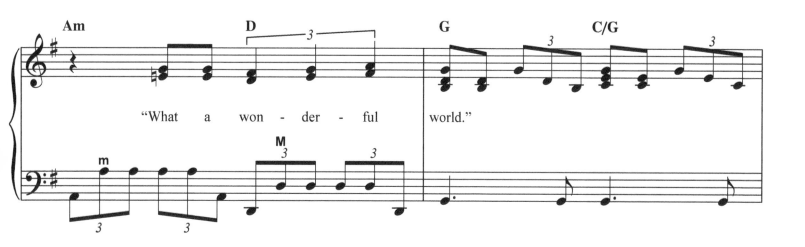

"What a won - der - ful world."

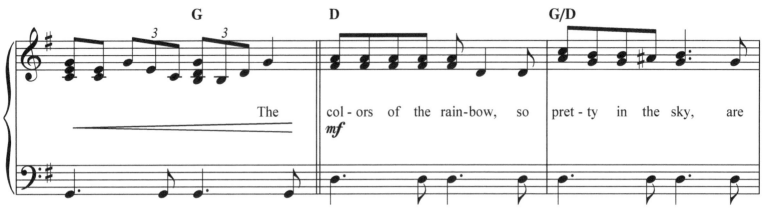

The col-ors of the rain-bow, so pret-ty in the sky, are

al - so on the fac-es of peo-ple go in' by. I see friends shak-in' hands, _____ say-in',

"How do you do?" They're real - ly say - in', "I love you." I hear

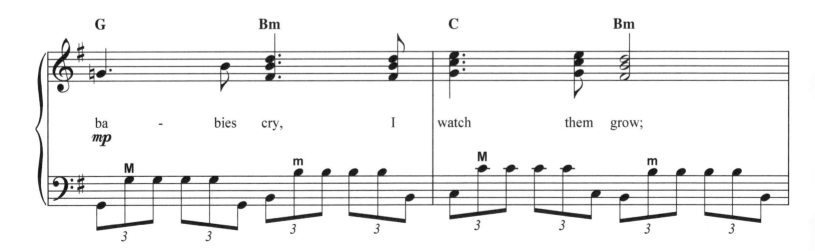

ba - bies cry, I watch them grow;

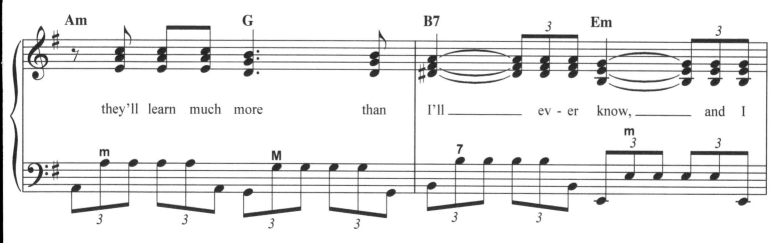

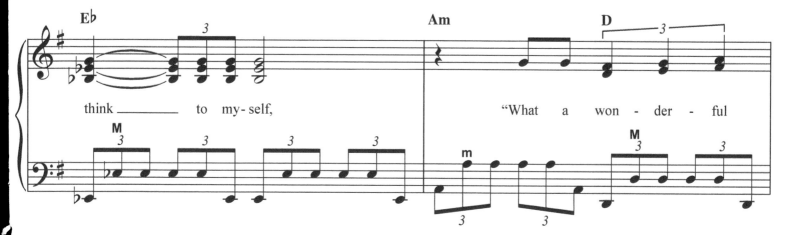

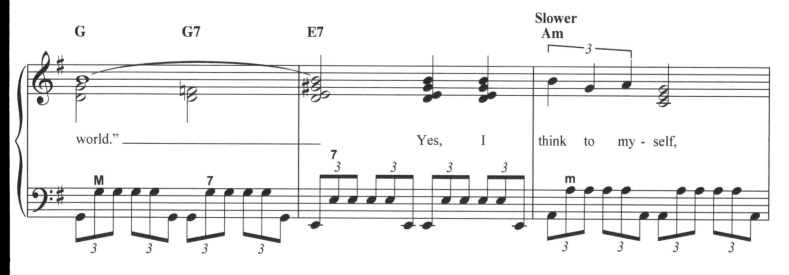

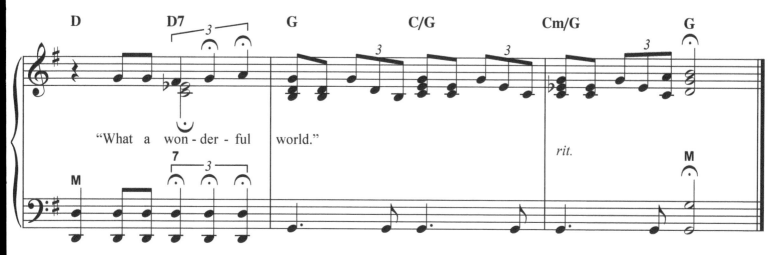

WITH A LITTLE HELP FROM MY FRIENDS

Words and Music by JOHN LENNON
and PAUL McCARTNEY

What would you think ____ if I sang ____
What do I do ____ when my love ____
(Would you be - lieve ____ in a love ____

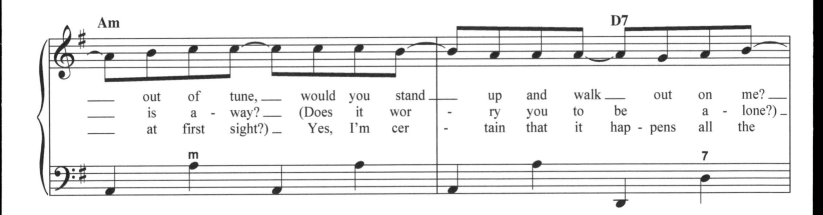

____ out of tune, ____ would you stand ____ up and walk ____ out on me?
____ is a - way? ____ (Does it wor - ry you to be a - lone?)
____ at first sight?) Yes, I'm cer - tain that it hap - pens all the

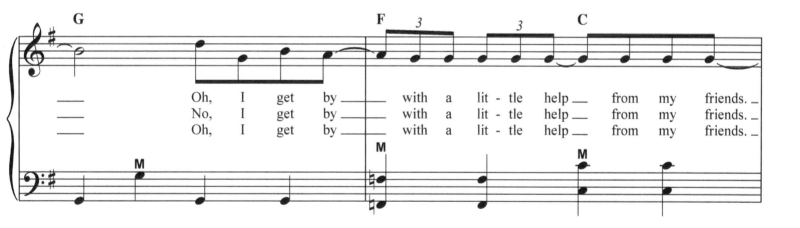

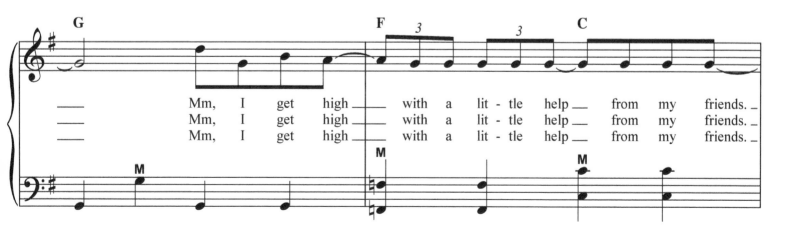

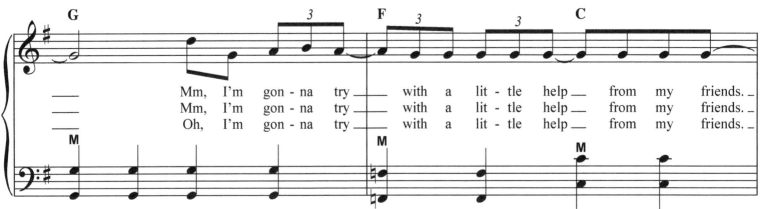

Mm, I'm gon - na try ___ with a lit - tle help ___ from my friends. ___
Mm, I'm gon - na try ___ with a lit - tle help ___ from my friends. ___
Oh, I'm gon - na try ___ with a lit - tle help ___ from my friends. ___

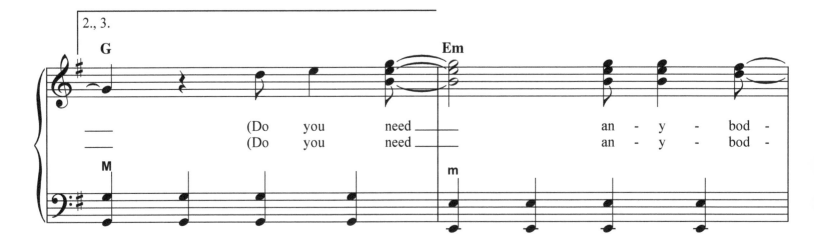

(Do you need ___ an - y - bod -
(Do you need ___ an - y - bod -

- y?) I need some - bod - y to love. ___
- y?) I just need some - one to love. ___

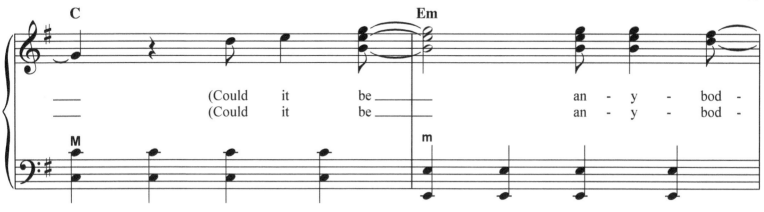

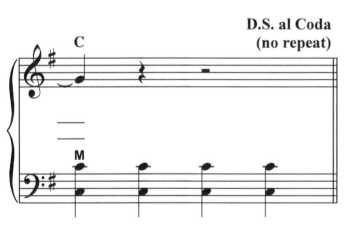

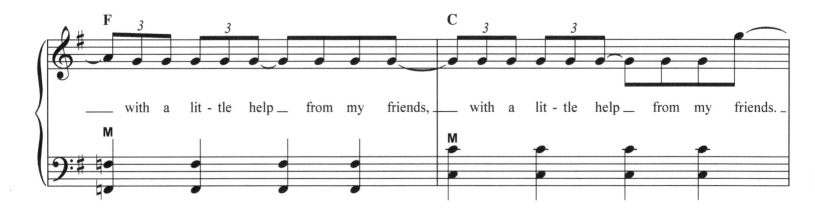

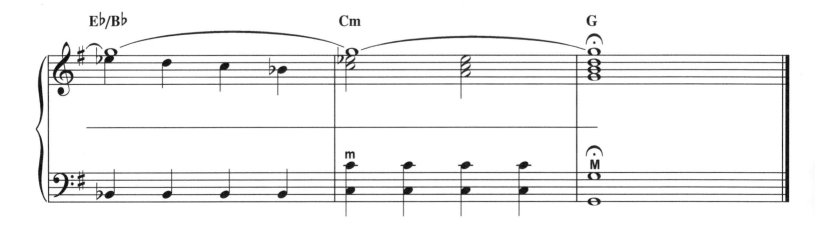